Ancient Egypt

The Ancient Secrets Revealed: Ancient Egypt, Gods and Pyramids

Simon Hawthornes

© Copyright 2015 by Simon Hawthorne - All rights reserved.

This document is geared towards providing exact and reliable information in regards to the topic and issue covered. The publication is sold with the idea that the publisher is not required to render accounting, officially permitted, or otherwise, qualified services. If advice is necessary, legal or professional, a practiced individual in the profession should be ordered.

- From a Declaration of Principles which was accepted and approved equally by a Committee of the American Bar Association and a Committee of Publishers and Associations.

In no way is it legal to reproduce, duplicate, or transmit any part of this document in either electronic means or in printed format. Recording of this publication is strictly prohibited and any storage of this document is not allowed unless with written permission from the publisher. All rights reserved.

The information provided herein is stated to be truthful and consistent, in that any liability, in terms of inattention or otherwise, by any usage or abuse of any policies, processes, or directions contained within is the solitary and utter responsibility of the recipient reader. Under no circumstances will any legal responsibility or blame be held against the publisher for any reparation, damages, or monetary loss due to the information herein, either directly or indirectly.

Respective authors own all copyrights not held by the publisher.

The information herein is offered for informational purposes solely, and is universal as so. The presentation of the information is without contract or any type of guarantee assurance.

The trademarks that are used are without any consent, and the publication of the trademark is without permission or backing by the trademark owner. All trademarks and brands within this book are for clarifying purposes only and are the owned by the owners themselves, not affiliated with this document.

Table of Contents

Introduction 1
Chapter 1: A Look at Ancient Egypt 2
    Before the Dynasties (c. 5300 – 3000 BC) 2
    The Primary Dynasties 4
    1st – 13th Dynasty (c. 3000 – 1650 BC) 4
    Intermediate Period 11
    14th – 25th Dynasty (c. 1650 – 664 BC) 11
    Late Period 15
    26th – 30th Dynasty (664 – 331 BC) 15
Chapter 2: The Numerous Gods and Goddesses of Ancient Egypt 18
    Ra 19
    Amun 23
    Isis 24
    Hathor 24
Chapter 3: The Regal Pharaohs of Ancient Egypt 26
    Tutankhamun 26
    Ramses II 32
    Ramses III 33
Chapter 4: The Beautiful Queens of Ancient Egypt 38
    Cleopatra 38
    Nefertiti 41
    Hatshepsut 42
Chapter 5: The Mysterious Pyramids of Ancient Egypt 50
Conclusion 54

Introduction

Ancient Egypt is full of mystery and wonder, with so much that can be taught to the modern day history buff. The ancient Egyptians had a fascinating civilization, and so powerful was this civilization that the effects of decisions made centuries ago are still being felt today.

Capturing everything about ancient Egypt could fill a library or several, but this book was designed to bring you the highlights of this period in human history and introduce you to the magic surrounding ancient Egypt. This book includes information on the lives of powerful Pharaohs, detailing their struggles as well as some insights into their might and eventual downfall.

Also included within the pages of this book are stories about the astounding queens of Egypt, renowned for the beauty, as well as their intelligence. There are some modern day mysteries, which are unraveled in this book.

As you read about Ancient Egypt, let yourself be transported back in time to a period of wonder, power, architecture and mystery. Find out about the ancient gods and goddesses that made up the religion of the ancient Egyptians, as well as the famous Pharaohs, beautiful queens and astounding architecture. Read on for a rich experience as we travel back to ancient Egypt.

Chapter 1:
A Look at Ancient Egypt

Egypt has a rich history, with tales of wealth and power from the Pharaohs, the fantasy that surrounds their gods and goddesses, architectural wonders, and interesting hieroglyphics. Additionally, the influence of Egypt is evident in our cultures today. As a cradle of civilization and one of the first world powers, Egypt was a critical territory to control for the ancient world. In order to understand the history of Egypt, it's important to analyze the major events in the dynasties and other periods.

Thanks in part to the dry climate of Egypt, many items, including pottery and human remains, have been preserved from these ancient times. Today, archeologists use these items to understand how these civilizations and cultures functioned, while piecing together the early history of humanity itself.

This section explores some these cultures and pivotal historical events briefly, putting them in the context of world history.

Before the Dynasties (c. 5300 – 3000 BC)

The ancient world of early Egypt was not based on a global community to the degree that we see today. While some trading was occurring between various communities, most of the emphasis was on food production. During this period, there was a shift in focus to agriculture from hunting and the nomadic lifestyle, with the Nile Valley being the primary source of food. It is believed that during this period, pits were discovered and used for the storage of grain. The ability to store food allowed for shifts in society to build wealth and the beginning of artistic endeavors.

As the transient lifestyle began to disappear, stationary communities were built. These communities took the social structures of their nomadic cultures and began to transition them into their new homes. As a result, social and cultural traditions began to appear in these villages and towns, including rites regarding the burial of the dead.

One such example was the Badarian culture, which showed evidence of social divisions. Within their burial grounds, those with wealth were buried in a separate area from others in the community. This culture also demonstrated one of the earliest rituals of burying the dead with their heads to the south and facing west, thus giving evidence that they believed in a land of the dead with its location somewhere in the west. Other later cultures also believed that a land of dead existed in the west and various rituals confirmed this fact.

These cemeteries have also yielded various pottery pieces, giving archeologists a key to understanding this early culture. The dead were buried in either matting or animal skins and often with jewelry or other personal belongings.

Additionally, goods found in these burial sites seem to indicate that the Badarian, while not nomadic themselves, did practice trading with other tribes throughout the Middle East and areas of Africa on their southern boundaries.

The Naqada culture soon followed, and it has been found that their burials reveal the first evidence of using linen for body wrappings. Additionally, their rituals and grave goods became more complex. This culture also demonstrated some of the early metalworking of Egypt, along with continuing to build trade routes throughout the Mediterranean, along with the Ethiopians and the Nubians to the south.

Yet, these early civilizations were just the beginning of what we know today as the Egyptian culture. The blending of rituals and social rites from various areas that these groups traded with became part of their cultures. Overtime, these were transmitted down into the more complex Egyptian culture, especially the rituals regarding the dead.

The Primary Dynasties

1st – 13th Dynasty (c. 3000 – 1650 BC)

Many leaps toward a standard governmental system came to life in the first dynasty. For example, evidence, including labels that indicated state goods, seems to suggest a system of taxation. This would imply a more complex governmental system, which was defined by rules for goods being traded and some form of currency. As part of this growth, hieroglyphic writing also began to show signs of standardization, thus producing one of the necessary foundations for a centralized government.

During the second dynasty, this central state came into effect. The Pharaohs consolidated their power using the political and economic foundations that had been built throughout the first dynasty. These early Pharaohs also began to fuse their religion with politics, so that Egyptians began to associate their rulers with the gods of their religion. Thus, the Pharaoh came to be revered as the ultimate authority in the region.

Trade was another means that was used by the Pharaohs to solidify their power. They enhanced their relationships with neighboring lands, such as Nubia, Palestine and Lebanon. This trade allowed them to build wealth, which helped to support a warrior class. Over time, this warrior class became revered in their own right, as they allowed the Pharaohs to expand their territory, gaining valuable land up and down the Nile.

The end of the second dynasty was marked by civil war, which ended with ascension of Djoser to Pharaoh, thus marking the beginning of the third dynasty. This dynasty also marked the beginning of what is known as the Old Kingdom. The Old Kingdom encompasses the third through sixth dynasties. It was during this period that Egypt was defined by the terms upper and lower. These designations were related to geographical positions in relation to the Nile.

During the third dynasty, the first big stone building was constructed as a burial place. This was also the start of what Egypt is most often known for, namely the pyramids. The first pyramid constructed during this time period are referred to as the Step Pyramid and was commissioned by Djoser. Other pyramids were also constructed during the approximately 75 years of this dynasty, which included 5 different kings.

The Golden Age of this Old Kingdom was the fourth dynasty. Trade flourished and the kingdom lived with peace and prosperity. Agricultural improvements resulted in greater yields. Additionally, construction of the pyramids moved forward. One such pyramid was the Great Pyramid of Giza, constructed by Pharaoh Khufu. Throughout this period, the capital of Egypt was Memphis. Each of the pharaohs during this dynasty was responsible for building a pyramid, thus historians often reference this as the era of pyramids.

One of the interesting parts of the period was that peace allowed for the growth of the arts, as well as significant architectural changes. Today, those architectural changes are apparent in the fact that pyramids from this era are smooth sided, versus the step pyramids of the third dynasty. It's also important to note that what is strongly associated with Egypt, the pyramids, were built to house pharaohs and other men and women of significance at the time of their death.

Pyramids are an intimate part of the royalty and religion of Egypt. These were part of the funeral rites, which could include goods and servants, thus allowing these Pharaohs to enjoy their afterlife. The rites of this period continued to develop and become part of the cultural norms of Egypt.

Additionally, the peace and prosperity of this dynasty allowed for a central government to flourish. How can we determine this to be the case? During this period of human history, there weren't construction crews or unions. Thus, pharaohs would use members of the lower classes or peasants to build these pyramids. In order to house and feed these individuals, the pharaohs built cities, thus creating records, storing goods and using strong governmental powers to organize society.

Artisans also moved closer to these centers of civic growth. Specialists included painters, priests, stone cutters and even mathematicians. Most of the work appeared to occur during the flood periods, when fields would be covered by the Nile. As a result, these peasants worked on construction projects during times they would otherwise been idle.

Records seem to indicate that each family was required to send one member to serve in a civic capacity. This did not automatically mean that family member was working on a building project. In many cases, this civic service could mean employed in a variety of areas, including libraries, temples and even festivals. These positions were not only held by men, but women were also assigned various duties. Those who were wealthier might hire someone to take their place, a tradition that has continued throughout history and other cultures. '

It's interesting to note that despite the fact that historically the pyramids have been pointed to as a large reminder of the slave labor that built them; records from the period appear to disagree. In fact, these pharaohs give the impression they had a willing public that built their pyramids. Most of these pharaohs were noted for their individual reigns and their personalities, versus their building projects, based on the records that have survived throughout the ages.

One of the last pharaohs of this dynasty appears to have been a woman by the name of Khentykawes, daughter of Menkaura. While it is not been confirmed that she ruled as pharaoh, finds within her tomb suggest that she may have ruled in this position.

Her tomb was built in the style of mastaba, which meant house of eternity or eternal house in ancient Egyptian. This was a flat roofed building in the shape of a long rectangle that would include several rooms. Khentykawes' tomb was made with two mastabas, the second one was not centered directly above the first because it would have been unsupported by the primary mastaba's open space.

Titles on her tomb had wording, which could be interpreted as *mother of the king of upper and Lower Egypt and king of the upper and Lower Egypt.* This wording, along with depictions of Khentykawes with the garb of royalty and the false beard that is typically associated with pharaohs.

This tomb was originally built in the niche architecture, characteristic of the time period, but these niches were later filled with limestone to create an even casing.

While pharaohs began to construct pyramids during the third dynasty, other members of the upper classes continued to build mastabas, some of which were found alongside the pharaohs' pyramids. (See chapter 5 for more on the mastabas and pyramids)

The Old Kingdom continued through the fifth dynasty. This time period is marked by changes in religion, especially the growth of the cult of the god Ra. By the end of this dynasty, Osiris had replaced Ra as the god of greater importance. Funeral prayers began to be written on papyrus and these were stored within the temples. At the same time, trade intensified and diplomacy with other cities and groups began to grow.

Still, by the sixth dynasty, the Old Kingdom was moving toward its end, as Pharaoh's lost power in favor of local officials who appeared to understand the people better. Thus, the integrated government that had existed throughout this period declined and eventually fell apart.

While the Pharaohs still held significant religious power, their political power throughout the seventh through tenth dynasties waned and saw the loss of territorial control, particularly Upper Egypt, around tenth dynasty. The local officials that stepped in during this time were found among the nobility, who had gained considerable authority and wealth throughout the earlier dynasties and began to exert this power politically.

During the seventh and eighth dynasties, as the central power disappeared, the pharaohs were known by little more than their names in a list. Historical references seemed to indicate that these pharaohs did not live long, perhaps due to ill health, but assassinations were also possible. Still these pharaohs were from the line of rulers during the sixth dynasty, but lacked the ability to maintain the controls that their ancestors had. Little is known about these kings, which were finally overthrown by one of the local officials referred to as nomarchs. Heracleopolis Magna was known as the nomarch who ushered in the ninth dynasty.

The ninth and tenth dynasties almost appear as lost dynasties, because little is known about these pharaohs. Egypt itself was broken into pieces and the central government was lost. Historians often group dynasties seven through ten as the First Intermediate Period, or a transition from the Old Kingdom to the Middle Kingdom. This period was also known for violence and conflict. Naturally, this brought about a reduction in trade as Egypt suffered from its internal strife.

Yet, during the eleventh dynasty, Egypt underwent some dramatic changes. For example, Mentuhotep II was the main ruler in the eleventh dynasty, and he managed to reunite Egypt. He re-formed the government through the use of appointed governors. Additionally, the government moved the capital from Memphis to Thebes. By the end of this dynasty, the Middle Kingdom had begun. As a result, the eleventh dynasty saw a return of Egypt to a center of influence, as the pharaohs of Thebes reclaimed Upper Egypt from the Heracleopolis Magna line of kings.

Egypt also reasserted its influence and in some respects, its authority, over the surrounding nations, particularly in Africa. Trade resumed in greater quantity and the pharaohs incorporated governors to assist them in reconsolidating their power and authority.

The Middle Kingdom covers the eleventh through fourteenth dynasties. The twelfth dynasty was known for its stability. In addition, during this dynasty, Egyptian literature continued to be refined. Papyrus copies of stories and books from this period have been found, indicating what was popular during this period. Building projects to the extent of the Old Kingdom were not as apparent during these dynasties, although the pharaohs continued to build tombs for themselves.

During the thirteenth dynasty, the kings saw relative peace, but their power continued to wane. Still they formed urban centers that indicated a period of growth and stability. While they ruled from Memphis, it is apparent that they also had loss of territory. As a result, the kings that made up the fourteenth dynasty ruled concurrently with some of the last kings of the thirteenth dynasty. Eventually, both lines of kings were overrun by the pharaohs of the fifteenth dynasty, known as the Hyksos from Western Asia. These rulers preferred to stay in northern Egypt, as they came from the northwest into the country. These pharaohs did not have complete control over the country, but the pharaohs of the thirteenth and fourteenth dynasties did not maintain their garrisons. Some records appear to indicate that the Hyksos took Egypt without any real fight.

This grouping of dynasties also appears to fall in a time period that can't be associated with the New Kingdom, but instead is part of the Second Intermediate Period.

Intermediate Period

14th – 25th Dynasty (c. 1650 – 664 BC).

The fourteenth dynasty had changes in the culture of Egyptians due to influences from Asia. Thus, the culture reflects Asian aspects within its religion and social norms. The Hyksos brought their storm god to Egypt and he later became associated with Seth, the Egyptian desert and storm god.

During the next several dynasties, there were distinct periods of overlap. While the Hyksos appeared to have conquered all of Egypt, by the sixteenth dynasty, there was a ruling class in Thebes. These pharaohs eventually expelled the last of the Hyksos kings during the seventeenth dynasty of the kings of Thebes.

Hyksos kings were truly demonstrative of the melting pot that was Egypt during this time period. While they were from Asia, other rulers throughout Egypt were from Canaan and other shepherding communities. African and Nubian influences were also apparent in the rulers of Egypt. As a result, the culture reflected the influence of these communities. Overtime, these communities had acquired enough time in Egypt that they themselves were referred to as Egyptians. Thus we see that Egypt was one of the first melting pots in human history.

Towards the end of the seventeenth dynasty, two kings expelled the Hyksos rule, thus unifying Egypt once more. The New Kingdom was the result of this unification and the eighteenth dynasty began.

The Book of the Dead has been part of movies made about mummies and has roots in ancient Egypt. But what is it really?

The Book of the Dead is actually a loose collection of texts and magic spells that were meant to usher someone through the underworld to the Egyptian afterlife. These were compiled over a 1,000 years and reflect changes in the Egyptian religion and the evolving of their faith.

Early pyramid texts provided historians with the origins of the Book of the Dead. Throughout the Old Kingdom and Middle Kingdom, these texts evolved into Coffin Texts, which depicted more individuals being able to journey to the afterlife, including more wealthy and noble personages. Combinations of these texts, along with newer spells were found in thirteenth dynasty. Royal family members, courtiers and wealthy nobles all had copies of the Book of the Dead included in their tombs by the nineteenth dynasty.

Typically, a copy of this book or texts with illustrations would be included in with the other funeral items as part of the burial rites. The Book of Dead was not standardized until the 25th or 26th dynasties, thus individuals adapted their own based on the texts available. These books are a great source of understanding for historians about how Egyptians viewed the afterlife during this period of dynasties.

Some of these texts were inscribed within the coffins themselves or on some of the wrappings of the mummies. So how did Egyptians view death and the afterlife?

Death was believed to involve a disintegration of the various modes of existence or aspects of being. Mummification was meant to preserve the physical body into an idealized form that included divine aspects. The Book of the Dead was part of this ritual, as it was said to include spells meant to assist in the preservation aspects of the dead. The heart was also protected with spells, because it was considered the source of intelligence and memory.

The life force remained in the tomb, thus it required sustenance. As a result, the funeral rites included offerings of food and water, meant to provide sustenance to the life force. Spells were also said to insure that the dead would remember their own name. If all the various aspects of an individual could be preserved and attended to properly, then the dead would live on as a blessed spirit with powers who could dwell with the gods.

As the dead traveled to the afterlife or Field of Reeds, a plentiful version of the living Egypt, they would also do manual labor as part of their time here. Then these dead individuals would dwell with the gods and eventually take on some of the gods' characteristics and thus acquire divinity for themselves.

Still, it was no cake walk to get to this glorious afterlife. The deceased would have a journey through gates, caverns and other areas that were guarded by different creatures. Spells in the Book of the Dead were meant to protect the dead from these creatures and any other threats.

Finally, as they complete their journey, their hearts must be weighed by Maat, goddess of truth and justice. If the scales balanced, then the dead individual had led a good life and could move on the afterlife. If the heart was out of balance, the afterlife of that individual ended quickly as another beast would eat the heart.

The Negative Confession, which is part of the weighing of the heart, reads like a divine enforcement of the everyday morality inherent in the Egyptian culture of the time. Still one could get into the afterlife, as long as the heart didn't feel compelled to confess to any indiscretions. The Book of the Dead included a spell meant to keep the heart from spilling any secrets, thus an individual could make it into the afterlife even if they hadn't been as pure as they claimed during their Negative Confession.

As we can see from this exploration of the Book of the Dead during these early dynasties, it was clear that moral and social norms were enforced through the religious aspects of the funeral rites. Individuals feared not attaining the afterlife and thus were willing to do whatever it took, including spells, offerings and mummification to achieve it. Within the economic aspects of Egypt at the time, burial was a big business, due to the amount of work involved to preserve and complete all the funeral rites. Even the poorest individuals still attempted to complete these funeral rites, especially the mummification process.

Pharaohs throughout the eighteenth to the twenty-second dynasties featured many important events as part of the New Kingdom. Temples were built and Egypt itself had seen tremendous growth.

The eighteenth dynasty also includes one of Egypt's most famous female rulers, Hatshepsut, who wore men's clothing while she was ruling. During this time, numerous temples were built and a large quantity of statues and other monuments were created. It was also during this dynasty that Tutankhamun would become king.

The nineteenth dynasty has the Pharaoh Seti I who brought back the old Egyptian religion. His predecessor had attempted to change Egypt's religion from a multi-god religion to the worship of a single god. Yet his conversion was not affective for the long term, as Seti was quickly able to reinstate most of the old traditions within a relatively short period time. His son Ramesses II succeeded on the throne and was also responsible for several large building projects throughout his rule.

Building and expansion of the ruling class continued throughout the next few dynasties. For example, the twentieth dynasty had Rameses III following in his father's footsteps when it came to construction. The twenty-first dynasty had building taking place at Memphis and Tanis.

The twenty-second dynasty features an important Pharaoh, Sheshonq 1 who expanded Egypt into her foreign territories. He was also in control of bringing back a more centralized political authority for the pharaohs.

Yet all these building projects and expansions of territory cost money and so trade also had to expand to cover the costs that the pharaohs were incurring. Yet, pharaohs began to find that they could not keep up with the costs of these projects and so many of the final pharaohs did not have such extensive building plans throughout their rules, but instead focused on revitalizing the historical temples of their ancestors.

Late Period

26th – 30th Dynasty (664 – 331 BC).

The late period reflected the end of the New Kingdom, as well as the end of the pharaohs themselves. During this relatively short period of time, pharaohs saw invasions and extreme upheaval within the ruling classes. Many pharaohs had short rules that were ended by murder or being disposed by a stronger political force. The instability left Egypt ripe for the picking as other world powers invaded and attempted to take over this beautiful country. This dynasty also saw the least amount of building projects, though there were a few new temples built. Instead most of the construction appeared to be focused on the rebuilding of older temples, particularly during the twenty sixth dynasty.

The twenty-seventh dynasty was marked by the invasion of King Cambyses of Persia, who established himself as Pharaoh. Despite his attempts at a peaceful transition, the Egyptians rebelled his rule. Thus, Egypt returned to its indigenous pharaohs, but the politics of the world were changing and Egypt was losing its position of authority within the ancient world.

The list of pharaohs during the twenty-ninth dynasty was long due to their relatively short reigns, with most of them being murdered or deposed within just a few years or months of beginning their reigns. By the thirtieth dynasty, Egypt's independence as a nation was in serious jeopardy. In fact, the last native Egyptian pharaoh ruled during this dynasty. His name was Nectanebo II.

Following the thirtieth dynasty, Egypt was invaded by Alexander the Great of Macedon, and the Greek government established the city of Alexandria. Upon the death of Alexander the Great, his empire was divided into three kingdoms which were the Macedon, the Ptolemaic Empire, and the Seleucid Empire.

Cleopatra, as the last Pharaoh of Egypt, fought with her husbands' Ptolemy XIII and Ptolemy XIV to retain control of Egypt. Yet, Roman influence continued and finally Roman forces made Egypt a tribute paying nation. Following Cleopatra's death, Egypt was officially made a part of the Roman Empire.

Yet while the history of ancient Egypt is extensive and mirrors many of the political and social upheavals that occurred during this period of human history, there is nothing that rivals their religion. Egypt's belief in its gods and goddesses withstood the test of time and their religion survived down through the dynasties, despite many political changes.

So what made up this religion that survived for thousands of years and still marks this amazing country even today? We can answer that by studying just a few of the gods and goddesses that were part of this country's belief system and it was these gods and goddesses that provided a framework for life and death in ancient Egypt.

Chapter 2:
The Numerous Gods and Goddesses of Ancient Egypt

Like various ancient civilizations, the Egyptians worshiped a large number of gods and goddesses. Each and every god or goddess represented something specific within their culture or nature, and all had a part to play in the day to day life and harmony of Egypt. There were approximately 2000 different gods and goddesses, each with their own cult that defined how they were to be worshiped. These cults would then create special holidays specific to their particular god or goddess. These holidays would become specific days of sacrifice or celebration and would fix these particular gods or goddesses into the minds and hearts of the people. While an individual Egyptian could not hope to worship every one of these gods or goddesses, it was not unusual for an individual to identify with a particular god or goddess and join their cult, directing most of their worship to that deity. However, the major gods and goddesses would typically be celebrated and worshiped by all Egyptians.

There were gods and goddesses who were responsible for natural elements such as the sun, rain and annual flooding of the Nile. There were gods and goddesses to cater to the people and those that handled issues in daily life. There were also gods and goddesses for animals and plants. Essentially everything that the average Egyptian could see and touch had an associated god or goddess. Thus, religion was a part of every facet of daily life, from the rising of the sun to the harvest.

Many of the gods had visual representations, which could be seen in artwork, through hieroglyphics or even sculptures.

Often, these gods and goddesses took a human form and combined it with a part of an animal or bird, typically the head. All Egyptians took the worship of these gods very seriously, and many kept representative idols or created shrines in their homes, which they used in their daily worship.

Some of the most recognized Egyptian gods and goddesses are described in this section. As you read, notice how the gods and goddesses of Egypt bear a resemblance to the gods and goddesses of both the Greek and Roman cultures. As you will see, many of the elements and processes of the nature and physical world was understood through these gods and goddesses, so representations of with similar themes were found throughout the ancient world's cultures and religions.

Ra

The sun itself was worshiped, as it was the source of light, warmth and of course, growth. In the ancient Egyptian religion, the sun was represented by one of the most powerful gods, Ra. This god was seen as a creator of both the physical world, but even humans themselves. In addition, Ra is said to have created other lesser gods, which also became part of the Egyptian lexicon.

Notice that like the Greek god Zeus, Ra was considered a leader of the gods and very powerful. Several gods and goddesses were created by Ra, namely Shu (god of wind), Tefnut (goddess of rain) and Sekhmet (the eye of Ra and an extremely violent goddess). Over time, Ra became associated not only with creation but also the underworld and the end of life.

Ra was associated with two boats, known as the morning boat and the evening boat. These boats were his means of travel through the sky and the underworld of Egypt (Duat). As with any god in the Egyptian religion, they were able to take on various forms. Ra, for instance, would ride through the sky in the form of a ram, but when in the underworld, he could visit or transform into his other various forms.

Ancient Egyptians believed that Ra sailed across the heavens through the day. His travel took place in a boat that was referred to as the 'Barque of Millions of Years'. This boat, however, was referred to using different names in the morning and at the end of the day. At dawn and in the early morning it was called 'Madjet,' which mean 'becoming strong.' At dusk or the end of the day, the boat was referred to as 'Semerket', which meant 'becoming weak.'

Since the rising of the sun was associated with rebirth, Ra became known as the god of rebirth and renewal. As a result, over time these legends helped to strengthen his role as a god of creation.

In his role as creator, legends appeared that spoke of how he created man from his tears. Those who worshiped Ra as part of his cult in Heliopolis believed man was created from Ra's tears. While Ra was believed to be self-created, others believed he was instead created by Ptah.

Additionally, Ra's blood resulted into two personifications, Hu (authority) and Sia (mind). He is also considered the creator of months, seasons, plants and of course, animals.

The form most associated with Ra is a man with the head of a hawk, a solar disk with a coiled serpent. Other forms were a man with the head of a beetle, ram, phoenix, heron, serpent, bull, lion or a cat. This is not the whole list, but as you can see

Ra is associated with a variety of animals, which represent a variety of characteristics.

The worship of Ra included the holiday known as Receiving of Ra, often celebrated on May 26 according to the Gregorian calendar. His cult grew from the second dynasty onward, pharaohs began to be seen as manifestations of Ra on earth. Eventually, Ra became a state deity, with a special bond to the Pyramids, Obelisks and the solar temples. By the fifth dynasty, Ra had received more of a connection with the underworld, particularly in texts that described the journey of pharaohs through the underworld to the afterlife.

By the Middle Kingdom, Ra took on greater associations with other gods, as we will explore shortly. Yet during the New Kingdom, Ra worship was complicated, with detailed text in various tombs specifically detailing his underworld walk. The idea of Ra aging with the sun also took on special significance during this period.

Christianity's growth in the Roman Empire ended Ra worship, turning it into just an academic pursuit by those who were formally priests.

A unique facet of Egyptian gods and goddesses was their ability to merge with other gods and goddesses, thus taking on a variety of characteristics beyond their normal abilities. For example, in the underworld, Ra would merge with Osiris (the god of the dead) and this made him in essence the god of the dead as well.

Ra merged with several other gods and these interconnections allowed for new entities to appear throughout Egypt's history.

One such combination was Ra with Amun, a god that was identified with the wind and creation of breath. As the cults of these two gods grew, they were combined to create Amun-Ra, what is known as a solar creator god. This combination appears to have begun sometime around the 5th dynasty, but really became a new state deity during the New Kingdom period.

Atum was a god closely linked to the sun and was referred to as the creator god. Along with Ra, both of these gods were regarded as father of pharaohs and were very widely worshiped. Ra-Horakhty was more of a title that linked Horus and the sunrise to Ra. Thus it appears that this combination is a reference to the journey of the sun.

Finally, Raet-Tawy came into existence as a female side of Ra and had little significance without him in the canon of gods.

As a creator of gods, Ra is specifically associated with the birth of several important goddesses. One was Bastet, the daughter of Ra and associated with his vengeance. She has also been represented by various cats throughout Egyptian history. Cats thus received a special significance in the eyes of Egyptian religion.

Sekhmet, another daughter of Ra, was also associated with his vengeance. She is known as being turned into a cow so she could not cause harm. As a result, cows also have special significance within the ancient Egyptian culture.

A myth involved two of these daughters of Ra, especially in his vengeance against mankind. Hathor was sent to kill mankind and her sister, Sekhmet, was sent to finish the job, but was tricked into drinking red beer. As a result, she was unable to complete the slaughter.

As you may have noted, these daughters of Ra were specifically associated with vengeance and being the arm of Ra, during times when he was angered with humans. Like other gods, Ra also had enemies or gods and goddesses that he struggled with. These relationships made for great legends and added an aspect of intrigue to the faith of these Egyptians.

Isis, the mother of Horus, wanted to have her son in a position of authority over Ra, so many stories depict her scheming against him to get the upper hand. Apep was the god of chaos and often referred to as Ra's primary enemy. It is the swallowing of Ra by Apep and his eventually spitting Ra back out that was used to explain the rising and setting of the sun.

While Ra is the one of the most famous Egyptian gods, other gods and goddesses played prominently in their religion. A few of them are discussed below.

Amun

Amun is also one of the most recognized and revered gods in ancient Egypt He was referred to as the 'King of the Gods'. He was the god of creation, in addition to being the god of life and fertility. His physical representation is usually of a man wearing a double plumed headdress, and also wearing a tunic or a kilt. An Ankh and Scepter are help in his right and left hands respectively.

For the royal family, Amun was an essential God. The royal family resided in the city of Thebes, where Amun was the patron saint. He was often identified as the father of the Pharaoh. In Thebes, several large temples were built to honor Amun.

As time passed, the Egyptians created an influential god they referred to as Amun – Ra. This god that emerged was a combination of Amun and Ra. He was considered as supreme, and the people called him 'one one.'

Isis

Possibly the most prominent goddess from Ancient Egypt is Isis. Isis was the wife or Osiris (god of the dead and resurrection) and the mother of Horus (a sun god). She was the goddess of fertility, marriage, medicine, and magic. Through Egyptian history, she was given many names which is possibly the reason she was known as the goddess with ten thousand names. Her visual representation was as a woman with a headdress that was shaped to resemble a throne.

In some depictions, she is wearing a vulture headdress while in others she has on a crown that has horns that surround a sun disk.

When it came to worship, she was primarily worshiped by women who were seeking her blessing for fertility. Men and women alike also worshiped her for protection, as they believed that she was able to conjure up magical spells that could help those who were in need.

Hathor

Hathor was a deity that was worshiped by everyone, be it royalty or commoners in ancient Egypt. She was the goddess of love. As a goddess, she was also worshiped for music and foreign lands. Her visual representation was that of a woman wearing a headdress that had two horns with a sun disk. The sun disk was encircled with a Uraeus between the horns.

As she was also a cow goddess, she is often depicted as a cow, or as a woman with the head of a cow. There is a large temple of Hathor which can be found in Dendera. She was often referred to as the Mistress of Dendera, as this place was said to be the center of her worship.

Some stories from ancient Egypt depict Hathor as the goddess who gave birth to the world. She is shown holding up the sky, and her legs are said to form the pillars that hold the sky up. She is similarly sometimes described as the eye of Ra.

Chapter 3:
The Regal Pharaohs of Ancient Egypt

In ancient Egypt, the Pharaohs were more than mortal rulers. They were also viewed as being deities, and for that reason they were very revered and looked up to. Pharaohs ruled over a period covering more than 30 dynasties through a time of three thousand years. In this period, there were more than 170 rulers of Egypt.

The law of succession in Egypt was for the son to take over from the father as Pharaoh. This happened most of the time though there were some instances where this could not occur.

Pharaohs ruled Egypt from the year 3150 BC, which stretches all the way back to biblical times. In 30 BC, the mighty Egyptian Empire was overcome by the Roman Empire, which brought an end to Pharaohs and their rule.

It was common place for the royal family to intermarry, with the rulers taking their daughters and granddaughter for wives, and sisters marrying brothers to ensure that the throne is kept within the family. However, even with these measures in place, the throne changed hands several times in ancient Egyptian history.

Of more than 170 rulers of Egypt, there are a few who stood out and live on through history books today. These Pharaohs shall be discussed in this section.

Tutankhamun

During the eighteenth dynasty, Egypt was reforming from the divisions that occurred during the thirteenth through fifteenth dynasties. One famous pharaoh from this time period is well known not for what he accomplished during his rule, but what was discovered in his tomb thousands of years after he died. King Amenhotep IV, in reversing religious changes made by his father, also changed his name to the one more well known today, Tutankhamun.

Amenhotep IV or King Tutankhamun was a particular Pharaoh of this dynasty that is also known by the name King Tut. His life, death and rule have been shrouded in mystery, one that has continued to fascinate scholars and historians of ancient Egypt to this day.

According to records that included lists of the kings from various dynasties, Tut was born in around 1343 BC when Egypt as a country was close to 2000 years old. King Tut was crowned as Pharaoh at the tender age of nine, and he ruled between the years of 1332 BC and 1323 BC approximately. He died while in his ninth year of rule, at the tender age of 18 or 19. During his rule, regents may have been in charge while the young king served as a figure head. This was not uncommon during this period, especially when adults didn't live for long periods of time and children could quickly be put in positions of power. Yet even for a pharaoh, this was a short lifespan particularly since this time period while it had some turmoil, also saw trade restored with countries that had been neglected under the reign of his father.

As was customary during this period of human history, he married his sister, Ankhesenamun. Royalty was often a family tree that curled back in on itself, with sisters and brothers being cousins and spouses as well. There is no evidence that he had any surviving children of his own. Evidence of two stillborn daughters has been found. But the inbreeding that continued throughout the royal families of Egypt may have resulted in genetic abnormalities that wouldn't allow the children to make it to full term. After all, King Tut's parents were full brother and sister themselves.

Historians have used the mummies found in his tomb to complete various genetic research to gain a greater understanding about the diseases and other physical information about royal Egyptians during that period of history. After all, the medical technology of today can explain illnesses and other disabilities that may have been considered acts of the gods during these dynasties.

Yet this king still made some significant changes during his short reign. He ended the ban on worship of Aman, giving back privileges to the priesthood of that god that his father had stripped away. King Tut also moved the capital back to Thebes from Akhetaten. But while he had to deal with battles from Nubians and other nations, so there was some evidence that he was not able to lead his troops into the actual battles because of disabilities and other issues. Again, historians surmise that genetic abnormalities due to the inbreeding may have played a part in the overall weakening of this particular king.

One of the mysteries that has intrigued historians for years is the burial site for Tutankhamun. There have been no records that provided any indication as to the burial of the king, let alone where his tomb may be located. This all changed in 1922 when an archeologist known as Howard Carter found what was later identified as King Tut's tomb, and within this tomb was the sarcophagus containing the mummy of King Tutankhamun.

Carter worked in Egypt for over 31 years before he found the famous tomb. At the age of 17, he was hard at work, serving as a copier of various wall scenes and inscriptions that were found within the pyramids and tombs. He built up his reputation to the point that he was appointed Inspector General of Monuments in Upper Egypt by 1899.

He resigned in 1905 and by 1907, Carter had become employed by Lord Carnarvon, an earl who spent his winters in Egypt for health reasons. Archaeology was a hobby to pass the time, but when he couldn't find anything himself, he decided to get more expertise. Hence, his partnership with Carter.

This pair worked together throughout World War I. When it ended, the pair began to work in the Valley of the Kings. They located evidence of King Tut, but this evidence didn't convince him that the tomb had been located. In fact, it spurred Carter forward to a specific area where he believed the tomb would be located. The determination of Carter to search the area down to the last stone was tested, when year after year passed with nothing to show for all his efforts. Finally, the earl decided that this was not worth funding for another season after five years of searching.

Still Carter was not willing to give up. He persuaded the earl to fund one last make or break season. In the winter of 1922, Carter was busy documenting exposed workmen's huts at the base of Rameses VI's tomb. After documenting all these huts, the team went down to the next level where they finally were rewarded for their persistence. The team found a step cut into the rock. But what the step led to was anyone's guess.

Freshly motivated, the team worked throughout the early part of November to uncover more stairs and the upper portion of an entrance, although it was blocked. The seals on the entrance weren't very readable, but it was apparent that this entrance led to a royal tomb. Carter wondered if it could be the tomb of King Tut. It could have also been a cache of mummies that had been relocated to preserve them from grave robbers and others who would disturb the dead in their final resting place.

Carter wanted to protect the find, so he covered the stairs back up and left guards, then went to make preparations to open the tomb. Three weeks later, Carter moved forward to opening the tomb with the earl at his side. When they removed the rubble for the second time, Carter was able to determine that the seals had King Tut's name on them.

The team determined that while the tomb was opened, it had not been emptied because it was resealed. Excited, they began the process of removing the seals and opening the tomb to see what they could learn about this king.

Although evidence was found that the tomb had been opened at least twice, they were able to determine that the robbers had not made it all the way into the actual burial chamber. Many of the obstacles Carter and his team encountered, appeared to have been put in place after the initial robbery of the tomb to protect against further desecration.

Yet in the end, this tomb proved to be a great discovery, because it shed light, not only on the rule of King Tut, but it also provided more detail about the time period of Egypt with its culture and rituals. Because so much was still intact at the time, this discovery also helped historians to solve different mysteries regarding the burial of pharaohs and the politics of the time period.

There was also a mystery surrounding the death of King Tut, with rumors of murder being the main cause of death. It took an international research team several years to discover the real cause. Unfortunately, the cause was not nearly as sinister as historians had expected. Various historians have speculated that the king fell off a horse and broke his left thigh in a few places. This injury did not heal properly and may have become infected. Since medical care at the time was nothing compared to what we have today, blood poisoning due to infection was not uncommon. The result of King Tut's injury was blood poisoning resulting from the open wound, and that blood poisoning is what likely ended up killing him. This king is also suspected to have had a bone disorder, which may have contributed to his demise by weakening his bones and making him more vulnerable to an injury that would not easily heal.

In the tomb of Tutankhamun, Carter's team found a variety of treasure, including gold, ivory and precious stones. There were over 3000 separate items retrieved, giving valuable insight into the burial practices of ancient Egyptians. These items also helped to build a better understanding of Egyptian culture and how important the rituals surrounding the pharaohs were to the fabric of society at that time.

An added mystery is attached to his tomb, in the form of a curse that was visited on those that disturbed his final resting place. Amongst the people who discovered his tomb, almost two dozen who were involved died under questionable circumstances. Until his tomb was discovered, mummies were thought to be magical and have healing powers, but since his discovery, mummies began to be associated with curses instead. Hollywood has contributed to this general belief with various mummy movies depicting a mummy attempting to destroy those who had disturbed its tomb or final resting place.

Ramses II

Ramses II was the third Pharaoh of the 19th dynasty. He was also known as Ramses the Great. In ancient he was one of the most powerful Pharaohs, and also one that made a significant mark in Egyptian history.

In his early twenties at around 1279 BC, he took over the thrown, and he ruled for 66 years until his death. He died from a range of natural causes, including health issues from arthritis. He is noted for his significant architectural achievements, including the temples of Simbel and Abu. There is also a memorial temple complex that was built during his rule known as the Ramesseum. He put up more Egyptian monuments than any other Pharaoh before or after him. Today, some of his architectural endeavors can still be seen in Egypt.

It is thought that Rameses II is the Pharaoh that is referred to in the Bible, particularly throughout the book of Exodus. This is perhaps because of his construction endeavors, which would have required a significant amount of manpower to come to fruition. The Isrealites were living in Egypt during this time period and the idea of slaves building pyramids and other construction projects grew because of this particular passage of the Bible. Yet historians have uncovered documentation that appears to support a compelled civic service that provided the labor for these projects. Additionally, the peasant class was pressed into service during the time periods when farming halted during flood season.

Rameses II had a large family, and he sired more than 100 children over his lifetime. He had several wives, more than what was considered normal at the time. This pharaoh managed to live more than most of the members of his family and was eventually succeeded by his thirteenth son who was named Merenptah. However, due to his legacy, his son continued to rule using his names, and so did another eight Pharaohs that were named after him.

His tomb was discovered in 1881, and his remains were moved to Cairo's Egyptian Museum. Depicted as a strong warrior, his mummy revealed fractures and wounds that were quite possibly incurred while he was in battle.

Ramses III

When discussing the mighty Pharaohs of Egypt, King Ramses III is thought to be the last of the greatest Pharaohs of Egypt. He was the second Pharaoh of the 20th dynasty and is thought to have held a considerable amount of power, particularly since this rule was marked by much turmoil, both politically from outside nations, but also economically.

Ramses took over the rule of Egypt upon the death of his father in 1187 BC. He ruled for more than 31 years. In order to closely identify himself with the gods, he was referred to by a large number of names with religious significance. These associations helped to bond him to his people and consolidate his political power.

The political climate of the time was chaotic, with Egypt constantly dealing with foreign invaders attempting to wrestle the wealth of the country away. During his fifth year of reign, Egypt was attacked on both land and sea by the Sea Peoples and Libyans. While Egypt was successful in fending off these attacks, although not being really great seaman themselves, these attacks marked the beginning of a period of intense internal strife and economic decline that would usher in the end of this dynasty.

Additionally, Egypt's influence in Asia also began to decline. The Sea Peoples, while defeated, began to settle themselves in Canaan and since the Pharaoh couldn't stop them, he decided to claim the idea as his own. Yet one of the most interesting developments that showcased the economic struggles was the labor strike that occurred during the 29th year of Ramses III's reign. The trouble started when Egypt could not fulfill its obligations to provide the food rations for them elite tomb builders and the artisans that lived in the village of Set Maat her imenty Waset.

Historians have been able to determine that a lack of sunlight, perhaps from an eruption, arrested the growth of the trees and impacted grain production for almost two decades. The result was food shortages and substantial increases in the prices of grain and other staples. This meant that the Pharaoh struggles to keep his workers fed as they continued his various projects. As we have discovered through our journey in ancient Egypt, the lack of understanding about how various natural cycles work, pharaohs could suffer the wrath of their people when things went amiss. After all, if you are a god that can't perform, then the people will get a god that can. So while the pharaoh carried much religious and political weight, they still could be plotted against and sent to the underworld, thus allowing a new son of Ra to be installed.

During the period that Ramses III was reigning, there was yet another strong focus placed on construction and development. By donating land to cult temples, more than one-third of all cultivated land belonged to these temples and their priests by the end of his rule. This was a dramatic shift of wealth as well, giving the priest a larger voice in the government and the social workings of Egypt. In addition, he was responsible for the construction of a mortuary temple which was known as Medinet Habu. To date, it is amongst Egypt's well-preserved temples. It was also one of the most well protected temples, with fortifications all around, thus indicating that times were not as peaceful as official monuments would have historians believe.

Additionally, the lack of a free press is evident, because Ramses III didn't make any mention of the difficulties he faced throughout his rule, instead focusing on his ambition to imitate his ancestor, Ramesses II. He also was clearly focused on presenting a public image of stability, even if that was not actually the case.

Ramses III died under mysterious circumstances, which was not uncommon during this period, and was buried in a massive tomb in the Valley of the Kings. It is suspected that he was assassinated, something that was found to be the case with many pharaohs, particularly those with extremely short reigns.

The conspiracy that surrounded his death was uncovered in papyrus trial transcripts. Here historians discovered that a royal harem conspiracy was concocted during the celebration at Medinet Habu. One of his wives, Tiye, apparently started the conspiracy and she stood to benefit if it was successful, as her son was the heir to Ramses III. He did in fact inherit and became Ramesses IV. This plot involved a large number of people, including the king's chief of the chamber, seven royal butlers, two Army standard bearers, royal scribes, treasury overseers and even a herald.

Unfortunately for these conspirators, they were found out and executed either by suicide through poison or being put to death by the state. Three different trials were held and at least 38 individuals were sentenced to die. Judges who were seduced by accused harem members in order to gain some advantage, but the judges involved were severely punished for falling for these tricks and it didn't appear to benefit the accused at all.

Tombs for Tiye and her son Pentaweret, another conspirator, had both of their tombs robbed and their names erased in order to prevent them from enjoying the afterlife. Thus, they were punished in life and also in death. Little is known of these conspirators except what can be gleaned from these transcripts. While the plot was uncovered and the trials occurred in the 32nd year of Ramses' rule, it is unclear if this was the plot that killed Ramses, although he did die in the same year that the trials occurred.

So how did Ramses die? It appears that his throat was cut in a lethal and deliberate fashion. This was determined by an examination of his mummy. Dr. Albert Zink from the Institute of Mummies and the Iceman in Italy was the examiner and he revealed a deep knife wound across the throat that reached the vertebrae and was not survivable. This wound was covered by the bandages around the throat and thus was missed for years. Before this discovery, many researchers believed that Ramses was killed using poison or other methods that would not have necessarily marked the body.

Ultimately the conspirators failed, because their designated king died as one of the conspirators and the heir designated by Ramses III was installed as the next Pharaoh.

So what were some of the marks that this particular pharaoh left on Egypt? The Great Harris Papyrus documents this pharaoh's vast donations of gold statues, monument construction and a variety of land donations. In addition, there were plenty of construction projects at a number of Egypt's temples as well as in other lands, such as Nubia and Syria.

Trading expeditions were documented as well, including one to the land of Punt, and the copper mines of southern Canaan.

Ramses III also began to reconstruct Karnak's Temple of Khonsu, based on foundations left over from the time of Amenhotep III. He also was able to finish the Temple of Medinet and decorated it with scenes of his various battles, both on land and sea. Today, this temple is considered one of the best preserved within the land of Egypt, as a monument to this ancient time period.

While the idea of curses regarding mummies really took off during the discovery of King Tut's tomb, Ramses III is regarded as the mummy most often referenced in movies and television shows. His tomb, while not necessarily found completely in tack, was also one of the largest located within the Valley of the Kings.

Chapter 4:
The Beautiful Queens of Ancient Egypt

Once one has considered the opulence, royalty, elegance and power that describes the mighty Pharaohs of ancient Egypt, due consideration must be given to the queens of ancient Egypt. They were of iconic beauty, and their style and grace are often the subjects of many Egyptian costumes used today. This in a sense, makes their beauty and grace timeless.

Yet, these queens were not only known for their beauty. Several served as pharaohs in their own right. Many went to battle and several queens held significant political and economic power. What makes this even more significant is that this was a time period when women did not hold rights equally with men. Obviously money and influence gave a woman more rights and abilities, but this did not necessarily filter down. Depending on the dynasty, some women held jobs as artisans and civic or governmental jobs.

So as we learn more about these amazing women, we can appreciate that not only were they known for their beauty, but they have to be admired for their political savvy and various building and economic accomplishments. With that being said, we introduce you to the last pharaoh of ancient Egypt and one of the most famous, a pharaoh by the name of Cleopatra.

Cleopatra

When discussing the queens of Egypt, Cleopatra is a name that will quickly come to mind. To this day, she is one of the most legendary queens of Egypt. She was the daughter of King Ptolemy XII, and she was born in 69 BC as his third child. Her elder siblings died before her father, which left her the rights of a firstborn child. For this reason, when her father passed, she became the last Pharaoh of Egypt. Yet, she was not of one of the indigenous ruling dynasties of Egypt.

Upon the death of her father who was the Pharaoh, she inherited the throne at the young age of 18 years old. According to Egyptian Law, she was forced to share the title of Pharaoh with her younger brother, because of her gender. Still she used her political savvy to push back against those individuals who were backing her brother, showing how a woman could rule such a large country with many outside forces working against her. Cleopatra lived with intrigue her whole life, both in dealing with Rome and the internal forces that for a time were able to remove her from power, but were not able to successfully end her political rule for good.

As a very intelligent young lady, she was able to lead the people of Egypt on her own. In fact, her rule also extended to an empire that included Cyprus, parts of the Middle East and sections in Libya. Cleopatra was a skilled linguist, as she was able to speak a total of nine languages. However, it is noteworthy that in her family, she was the only one who could speak the Egyptian language. She was also conversant with Egyptian religion and ensured that she identified herself as a modern version of the goddess Isis.

Cleopatra stood out because she was exceptionally beautiful. She was also charming as a leader, and known to be persuasive with her people. Her rule was brought to an end by her brother who was eight years younger than her (and who also held the title of her husband) when he exiled her to Syria in 48 BC because he felt she was too independent.

The build up to her exile took several years. Following the first year of her reign, she took advantage of her brother's youth by removing his name from all official documents. From that point onwards, her image and name appeared on all legal tender. Cleopatra continued to rule without her brother's input, which in turn upset court officials as she proved to be difficult to control. With her brother in the grip of court advisors, there was a plot hatched to overthrow her so that he could take over, and in effect, be controlled by them.

The Roman Empire was gaining more power at the time, and in a bid to get back to her throne, she took both Julius Caesar and Mark Anthony as her lovers for a period of time. However, the land of Egypt was overcome by the Roman Empire.

Later, Cleopatra regained control of her throne, while ending her exile upon the death of her brother, and in 46 BC she had her first son. The father of the child was Julius Caesar, giving her a political edge with the Roman Empire. Yet her political manipulations could not keep Egypt independent of Rome and although she was connected with several powerful men, she was powerless in the end to stop Roman troops from marching through her country. She herself was considered a war trophy. Cleopatra passed away as the last reigning pharaoh of Egypt. It is believed that she committed suicide after the death of Mark Antony, her lover. After the conquering of Egypt by Rome, the nation paid tribute to Rome and did not again have any pharaohs.

Yet the country itself has continued to this day and remains largely intact with much of its culture still available for others to study and learn from. This cradle of human civilization has preserved much of its early history and so even these queens are still remembered and discussed for their abilities and accomplishments.

Nefertiti

Over the years, sculptors have created busts to mimic the likeness of Nefertiti. She was a famous Queen of ancient Egypt and was the wife of Akhenaten during the 18th Dynasty. This particular queen was a woman famous for her delicate beauty and yet her life is also shrouded in mystery, both about the origins of her family and where she is buried.

She and her husband were in power at a time when there was immense wealth in the kingdom of Egypt. At that time, her husband was intent on changing the religious practices of ancient Egyptians. He put an end to the worship of old gods and introduced a new national god to be worshiped. This god was known by the name Aten. Various sources appear to support the idea that she prominently reinforced the religious ideas of her husband. Yet, when her husband passed, the nation was quickly returned to its original religious roots by the next pharaoh, who was her step-son.

There are certain aspects of Nefertiti that are clouded in mystery. The first is that to date, no one has been able to identify where this queen originated from. There are theories which say that she was a foreign princess while others say that she was the daughter of Amenhotep III, and one theory states that she must have been a member of Egypt's elite.

The second mystery revolves around her death. To date, it has not been possible to locate her remains. Due to changes in the royal family in the 13th year of Akhenaten's reign, information about royal women is missing from the records and amongst those with missing information is Nefertiti, the queen. Around this period of time she passed away, so there is limited information about this particular queen. Some historians believe she may have even ruled as pharaoh for a time after her husband passed away, although this is not confirmed.

By the time Nefertiti had passed away, she was the mother of six daughters. There is no evidence to indicate that she had ever given birth to a son.

Much more information is available about a pharaoh from the eighteenth dynasty, a woman by the name of Hatshepsut.

Hatshepsut

Queen Cleopatra and Queen Nefertiti were both renowned for their beauty. However, Queen Hatshepsut was famous for dressing in men's clothing in a bid to prove that she was worthy of the title of Pharaoh.

As the fifth pharaoh of the eighteenth dynasty of Egypt, she was officially considered a co-regent with her half-brother, who later became her husband. This husband passed away, leaving her a regent with a very young nephew. Yet, this pharaoh refused to be sidelined during her reign, but took on the title of king. She took on all the duties and responsibilities of a pharaoh, at a period of time when women rarely took on this type of rule. As we will see, there were few examples available for Hatshepsut to model her own reign after. She appeared in men's clothing but also took to wearing the fake beard that other pharaohs had done throughout the ages. At the same time, she blazed trails and is still one of the most well-known indigenous female pharaohs of ancient Egypt.

She ruled for roughly 15 years and historians believe she was one of the more successful pharaohs. Hatshepsut reigned longer than any other woman from one of the indigenous ruling dynasties.

After 15 years of ruling successfully, she mysteriously disappeared. It is suspected that her nephew plotted for her death upon his coming of age so that he could take over the throne. He was named Thutmose III, and he took over the throne immediately it was realized that she had disappeared.

This pharaoh established trade routes and recreated networks that had been disrupted the rule of the Hyksos. One of her trading expeditions was to Punt, during her ninth year of reign. The expedition started out with five ships, which returned with a large number of trade goods, including frankincense and myrrh, two very famous spices of those ancient time periods.

The returning delegation brought back live trees in an attempt to transplant foreign trees onto Egyptian soil. Charred frankincense was ground into kohl eyeliner, one of the first recorded uses of resin.

While little is known about other trade expeditions, beyond the fact that they did occur, it seems that this pharaoh did also lead military campaigns, targeting Canaan and Nubia. Yet overall, her rule is documented as peaceful with most of Egypt's neighbors.

Hatshepsut also wore an architectural hat during her rule in Egypt. According to historians, she commissioned literally hundreds of building projects throughout both the upper and lower parts of Egypt. In fact, her projects were so grand in both detail and number that later pharaohs attempted to claim her construction projects as their own. Her architect Ineni had worked for her father, husband and their royal steward. Thus, her projects had a sense of continuity with the previous rulers in her immediate family.

Statues were also produced in great quantity during Hatshepsut's rule. As a result, many museums today include a statue from her time on the throne of Egypt. The Metropolitan Museum of Art in New York City, for example, has a room that they have dedicated to the statues and other pieces from the Hatshepsut ruling period.

As with other pharaohs, Hatshepsut was in the business of creating monuments. Many pharaohs believed in building as much as possible to secure their legacy in Egypt over time. So it is no surprise that Hatshepsut followed this tradition. We mentioned her numerous construction projects, but there were a few that really stood out. One was the restoration of the Precinct of Mut. This ancient goddess of truth and justice has seen her precinct ravaged and defiled by foreign rulers during the 15th dynasty of Hyksos rule. Parts were also taken by other pharaohs to be used in their various building projects. This pharaoh thus had twin obelisks erected at the temple's entrance. One of those obelisks is still standing today, one of the tallest surviving ancient obelisks, but the other one was broken into two pieces and had toppled down as a result.

She had other pet projects. One such construction project was the Red Chapel, which may have been intended to serve as a baroque shrine between the two incredibly high obelisks in the Precinct of Maat. This shrine was lined with stone carvings used to illustrate a number of significant events that occurred during Hatshepsut's life.

Her love of obelisks meant that she had several constructed, including two that were made to celebrate the sixteenth year of her reign. However, one of the original obelisks was broken during the quarrying period, so a third was carved to replace the broken one. At the same time, the broken one was simply left in the quarrying site because it was no longer useful.

Historians are thankful for this, because they were able to use this unfinished obelisk to gain a better understanding of how these obelisks were quarried and created.

There is also evidence of how these large pieces were carefully moved. In talking about all the construction of this particular pharaoh, it is important to note that all of these projects were completed without the use of any modern machinery. Take a moment and think about how much work and organization that was involved in executing these construction developments throughout all the dynasties of ancient Egypt. These were large, detailed and technical projects. So it required planning and large numbers of workers in order to complete them. Yet, all this work was achieved without cranes, large trucks, bulldozers or other heavy machinery.

Temples were another source of construction during her reign. One such temple was located at Beni Hasan, known as the Temple of Pakhet. Bast and Sekhmet were similar war goddesses, so their names were combined into Pakhet and the temple's location was in an area that bordered both their cults' territories.

The temple was built into a cavern underground on the eastern side of the Nile. The construction was so well thought out that the temple received admiration from Greeks during their occupation of Egypt during the Ptolemaic Dynasty. These goddesses were much admired by the Greeks because of their similarity to the Greek goddess Artemis.

This temple appeared to have been built in a neighborhood that included several other more ancient temples, but unfortunately it does not appear that any of those temples have survived into present day. One of the interesting parts of this temple is the long dedication text that includes the equivalent of a political speech against the Hyksos given by Hatshepsut. She is seen as starting a revival of Egyptian culture and tradition that was ravaged and saw a decline during the Hyksos period of rule.

Seti I, a pharaoh during the nineteenth dynasty, appreciated the work of the temple so much that he attempted to claim it as his own and tried to wipe Hatshepsut's name from the walls.

Yet probably her greatest project was the one that most pharaohs spend their entire rule creating, her tomb. This complex was placed on the West Bank of the Nile, near the entrance of what later became known as the Valley of the Kings. It was as if she saw the beauty of the location and first planted her roots there. Overtime, other pharaohs followed, attempting to imitate her grandeur in their own complexes and pyramids.

The focal point of her complex was a colonnaded structure that rivaled the Parthenon for its symmetry. What makes this structure even more impressive is that it was built almost one thousand years before the Greek Parthenon. Terraces were also designed to take advantage of the surrounding cliffs and featured lush gardens throughout.

With all these projects, trade expeditions and other efforts, it is clear that this was a pharaoh to be acknowledged and celebrated. During a time when most women did not enjoy many or any rights of their own, this woman ruled a world power and managed many impressive feats within a relatively short period of time.

So how does Hatshepsut stack up to other female rulers throughout Egyptian history? While it might not have been the norm in ancient Egypt, women did rule throughout its history. Many did so as regents for their sons or other relatives that were deemed not yet old or experienced enough to handle the job of ruling the nation.

One such regent was Merneith, who lived during the first dynasty. She was buried with all the honors accorded a pharaoh and it appears that she may have ruled for a time on her own. Nimaethap acted as a regent for her son Djoser, who later ushered in the fourth dynasty. Again, she also ruled for a time as pharaoh in her own right. The last pharaoh of the sixth dynasty may have been a woman, according to historians, who have found her name in the Histories of Herodotus and the writings of the Egyptian historian Manetho.

During the twelfth dynasty, formal power over both the upper and lower areas of Egypt was assumed by Queen Sobekneferu, almost three centuries before Hatshepsut came onto the scene. Ahhotep I was known as a warrior queen, serving as a regent during the reigns of her two sons just prior to Hatshepsut's dynasty. Overall, these are just a small sampling of the possible women rulers sprinkled throughout Egypt's history, but these women are part of the group of indigenous Egyptian dynasties. Cleopatra VII was the last known pharaoh of ancient Egypt, but she was not a member of an indigenous Egyptian dynasty.

As we can see, Egypt's ruling was not limited to men, but of all these women, Hapshepsut's reign appeared to have been the longest with a significant period of prosperity for the people. In areas of war, she was successful early on in her rule, but this led to a relatively peaceful era. Trading relationships were reestablished and as we have seen, numerous building projects were funded from these trade agreements. Her rule was marked by an architectural standard that wasn't rivaled by any other culture or world power for almost one thousand years after her rule ended.

One of the customs of pharaohs was to toot their own horn, so to speak. There was no such thing as a press back then, so pharaohs had to serve as their own press agents. Thus, they made sure their names were on all their construction projects, building, statues and temples. While the buildings gave Hepshepsut plenty of opportunities to draw attention to herself, it also demonstrated how successful her trading agreements were. After all, construction takes money and without the successful trading efforts, she would have not been able to fund these projects.

The country as a whole prospered under her rule, as evidenced by the relative peace that accompanied it. Still, one can't stop political intrigue and so many historians believe she was killed or made to disappear in order to make way for her nephew, who had served as her co-regent.

While women in the nobility had high status and were able to inherit and will property to individuals, a woman ruler was still relatively rare. Twosret, a woman pharaoh from the end of the nineteenth dynasty, may have served as the last indigenous pharaoh after Hepshepsut. In ancient Egypt, there was not a word to describe a queen regent, so king was applied to the ruler regardless of gender.

Hapshepset was not the first to take on the title of king, but she was definitely one of the best trained women for the post. She served her in a powerful office during her father's rule and it was clear that she was not weak queen during her husband's reign. As a result, she had plenty of administrative experience and was well prepared to take on a pharaoh's duties. Her rule was not challenged and it appears that it was not until her death that her co-regent really took on any major responsibilities, beyond his heading the Egyptian army of the time. Additionally, by taking on the traditional dress of a pharaoh, Hatshepsut asserted her right to rule as the king, versus being a Great Wife or Queen Consort. The highly stylized beard was typical of all pharaohs, regardless of gender.

Additionally, the lack of representation of Hatshepset with obscured breasts was not in an attempt to hide that she had been a woman, but instead these depictions showcased the symbols of the office, which had religious significance. Thus, it was more important that these were correctly displayed before worrying about giving a gender specific representation of the ruling pharaoh.

Hatshepsut used the ability of pharaohs to write her own history, which includes legends about her birth and the fact that she indicated her father had always meant for her to rule. Still as a successful pharaoh, she clearly had the support of her people and it appears that she was a capable ruler.

As we move from the queens of Egypt, this particular queen's extensive building leads us right to the most important part of Egypt's mark on the world and that is the pyramids themselves. While ancient Egypt's culture and society has passed away, these tombs that were constructed for their rulers and the noble class have given us many clues to how they lived and how they died, what was valuable to them both politically and religiously.

Chapter 5:
The Mysterious Pyramids of Ancient Egypt

The Egyptian Pyramids are a key attraction in Egyptian history and bring plenty of tourism dollars to the shores of Egypt every year. These tombs add beauty to Egypt's desert landscape, while serving as a stark reminder of how ancient this country truly is. The number of Egyptian pyramids is still unclear, but it assessed to be 118 currently. Majority of the pyramids have been built to be used as tombs for ancient Egyptian Pharaohs and members of the noble and ruling classes. The oldest pyramid is called the Pyramid of Djoser, which was built in 2630BC-2611BC.

The Pyramid of Djoser is a stepped Pyramid. This early design is different from most of the other later pyramids. It is 203ft high and has a base of 411ft, but the sides are not smooth at all. Yet as buildings progressed throughout the dynasties, the steps were internalized and the sides themselves became smooth, which is what most people think of when they think of the pyramids.

In Giza, you can find the most famous of all the pyramids; among these is the pyramid of Khufu. In addition to being the tallest pyramid in Egypt, the pyramid of Khufu is one of the Seven Wonders of the World. It is 455ft tall and has a base of 756ft. The other two pyramids of Giza are the pyramid of Menakuare and the pyramid of Khafre. The place to find the most pyramids is Saqqara. There are 17 pyramids there.

In 1842, Karl Richard Lepsius came up with the first modern list of pyramids, where he recorded 64 pyramids. Several more had been identified by 2008, bringing the estimated total to

118. The location of pyramid 29, which is named the headless pyramid, was lost for a second time because it was buried in sand, but it was found again during an archeological dig in 2008.

The Red Pyramid is very popular due to its unique red color. But how did they manage such a unique color for such a large building? Quite simply, they built this particular pyramid with a unique red limestone, thus giving this particular pyramid its standout look. With a height of 344ft, and base of 722ft, it is the third tallest pyramid, following Khufu and Khafra. This particular pyramid used to be covered with white limestone, but the limestone was removed to help build the surrounding city. The Pharaoh Sneferu commissioned this structure as the third pyramid to be designed and built during his rule.

The Black pyramid is an exceptional pyramid due to its size and outstanding color. It was constructed by King Amenemhat III between 2055-1650 BC. This particular pyramid is 246ft high and has a base of 344ft. The pyramid was originally named "Amenemhat is Mighty", but then the pyramid earned the name the "Black Pyramid" for its dark look, like a mound of rubble. There were originally eleven pyramids in Dashur, and this is one of the five which still remain down to this day. It was the Black pyramid which was the principal pyramid where both the Pharaoh and his wives were buried.

King Amenemhat II made a pyramid identified as the White pyramid. It can be found in Dashur. However, the pyramid is in ruins with nothing but its limestone left to be seen. The rooms and other areas of the pyramid have been destroyed over time. Still it is interesting to note that builders used a variety of limestones to achieve different colors and designs that made these pyramids stand out among their neighbors.

One of the most important things to note about these pyramids is how much they tied into the ancient religion of Egypt. So much of Egyptian life revolved around the gods and goddesses, especially the afterlife. Whole groups of individuals were involved in the process of burial and mummification, which meant that these pyramids also stood as symbols of the afterlife.

Kings and queens, as well as nobility, had these large tombs built to reflect their beliefs in the afterlife. As we discussed, the Book of the Dead was key to helping the dead complete their journey to the afterlife in a preserved state. Yet, the Book of the Dead was not limited to the wealthy. Evidence has been found that even the poorest individuals attempted some type of mummification and used the spells to help their loved ones make it to the afterlife.

When it comes to pyramids, the mastaba style was prevalent from the first dynasty, but had largely disappeared by the 18th dynasty, making way for the pyramids with the triangle type appearance that most individuals are familiar with today.

The mastaba began as a simple building with just a few rooms in a layout similar to a home. The individual's sarcophagus (coffin) would be placed in the central room with surrounding rooms filled with funeral offerings. During the next few dynasties, the mastabas evolved, with the central room being sunk down into the ground. Stairs and other platforms were used to connect the various rooms of the mastaba.

Grave robbing was not uncommon during these periods of Egypt's history. Thus, the designers of the mastabas and the pyramids began to create shafts and other elements meant to deter theft. Some rock cut tombs also began to appear during this time period in an attempt to stop theft. Religion also played a role in deterring these thefts, as pharaohs continued to grow into their central role within society as living gods.

For the mastabas, an offering room and a specific shaft were built into the overall design. By the fifth dynasty, this design shifted the actual burial room under the south side of the mastaba, while creating columned rooms and slanting passageways. Mastabas themselves had disappeared by the 18th dynasty, replaced by an independent pyramid like chapel over the burial room itself.

So why was grave robbing so prevalent? In large part, it was due to the funeral goods themselves. Pharaohs and the wealthy upper classes would send their dead off to the afterlife with what could be considered a lifetime's worth of riches in the form of jewelry and other items. For the poorer classes of Egypt, this was extremely tempting, even though there were superstitions and fears associated with disturbing the dead.

Conclusion

As you reach this section of the book, you have just completed a short journey through this incredible period of human history. Ancient Egypt is fascinating, and this book has attempted to give you deeper insight into the key players and influencers of ancient Egyptian civilizations. We also hope that you can begin to see how these influences have continued to flow down into modern history.

The fact that the Great Pyramid of Giza built thousands of years ago, but can still be referred to as one of the Seven Wonders of the World today speaks volumes about the Egyptians, their building techniques, and architectural expertise.

By reading about the Roman Empire and their influence in Egypt, one understands why there are no Pharaohs ruling Egypt to this day. Also, the details of the discovery of King Tut's grave should help you piece together certain myths, particularly about the myth of kings being buried with their immense treasures.

The book also contains information that explored how the royal family operated, giving you a greater understanding of their reasons for intermarriage and succession. This should shed some light on why there were several very young Pharaohs, and also, on how women who were on the throne were treated.

Ancient Egypt featured beautiful women with excellent intelligence and political savvy, as well as powerful Pharaohs who changed the landscape of the sands, and gods and goddesses whom the people depended on for help and consistency in every aspect of their lives. Now that you have completed this book, you know more about their lives, their humanity, and you can understand the reason why to this day, they have not been forgotten.

*****Free Bonus*****

Ancient Rome

The Roman Republic - Rise of the Roman Empire and Roman History - Introduced

Table of Contents

Introduction	58
Chapter 1: The Rise of the Roman Empire	59
Variations of the Myth	60
Benefits of the Palatine Hill	60
Chapter 2: The Roman Kingdom	62
The Kingdoms	62
Romulus	62
Numa Pompilius	63
Tullus Hostilius	63
Ancus Marcius	63
Lucius Tarquinius Priscus (Lucius Tarquinius the Elder)	64
Servius Tullius	64
Lucius Tarquinius Superbus (Lucius Tarquinius the Proud)	64
Chapter 3: The Republic	66
The Early Republic	66
The First and Second Triumvirate	67
Chapter 4: Building the Empire	69
The Julio-Claudian Dynasty	69
Flavian Dynasty	70
Chapter 5: The Peak and Beginnings of Decline	72
The Nerva-Antonine Dynasty	72
Severan Dynasty	73
Conclusion	76

Introduction

The ancient Roman civilization has fascinated historians for centuries because they had one of the largest empires the world has ever seen. At the height of its power, it covered 2.5 million miles and stretched from England to North Africa, Asia Minor and parts of northern and eastern Europe.

Despite its humble beginnings as a collection of settlements around the river Tiber, the Roman Empire contained between 50 million and 90 million people at its peak. This is equal to about 20% of the world's population at the time.

The Roman Empire survived for 12 centuries and saw three different forms of government. It began with a monarchy in around 753 BC. The first kings were overthrown about 200 years later, and the empire ran as a republic. However, in 27 BC, the Roman leader Octavian adopted the name, Augustus, signaling the beginning of the Autocratic Empire.

Roman civilization has helped shape modern politics, government, law, literature, art, engineering, architecture, technology, warfare, language, religion, and society. The Romans were technologically advanced for their time, with an advanced road system and a system of aqueducts. They also built large palaces, monuments and public facilities that still stand today.

In this book, we shall look at some of the highlights of the Roman Civilization, from the Res Publica system of government that has inspired modern governments, to the mythology and religious beliefs of the period. However, before we dive into the deep end, we need to start from the beginning and learn about the origins of the Empire.

Chapter 1:
The Rise of the Roman Empire

There are many different stories about the origins and establishment of the Roman civilization, many of them now classified as myths and legends. The most famous of these myths is the story of Romulus and Remus, the twins who were raised by a wolf. This story had to be merged with another myth, the epic of Aeneid by Virgil, which tells the story of the Trojan prince Aeneas and how he became the ancestor of the Romans.

According to the myth of Romulus and Remus, they were twin boys born of the Princess Rhea Silva and Mars, the Roman god of war. There was a prophecy that proclaimed the twins would overthrow their great-uncle Amulius, who had overthrown their grandfather Numitor for the throne, and, for this reason, Amulius ordered their execution. However, as is the case with many mythical heroes, the twins were spared by the servants who were told to kill them and were instead abandoned on the banks of the river Tiber.

The twins were found and nursed by a female wolf until a shepherd called Faustulus found them and adopted them. The shepherd and his wife raised the two boys as if they were their sons, and when they were adults, they carried out the prophecy and restored their grandfather Numitor to the throne.

The twins decided to set up their own city, and it is at this point that Romulus and Remus disagreed. During the quarrel that followed, Romulus killed his brother and founded a city called Roma (Rome) which he named after himself.

The city grew very quickly, refugees from around the region flooding into the city. Most of the refugees were male and unmarried, and soon the new city was full of mostly men and very few women. To even the numbers, Romulus organized an ambush of the neighboring Sabines. The short war that followed this directive led to the Sabines agreeing to join the Romans to live as one.

Variations of the Myth

There are several variations of this origin myth. In one of them, Hercules seduces Rhea Silva. In another version, Amulius orders Rhea Silva and the twins to be thrown into the river Tiber.

In all these accounts, one thing that remains constant is the servant that feels sorry for the children and spares their lives. Other things that stay constant are the fact that both boys grew up as shepherds, and that Romulus was saddened by his rash actions and buried his brother with respect and regret.

Archeologically, the Latins settled on the Palatine Hill and its surroundings from about 1000 BC. Despite the fact that these early settlers were very few and hardly organized, they still managed to grow into one of the most powerful civilizations known to man. This is partly due to the positioning of the city itself, and partly due to the neighbors that those early settlers had at the time.

Benefits of the Palatine Hill

The Palatine hill was ideal for the settlers, as it was very close to the sea making it an ideal location for trade and commerce. The larger geographical area was guarded by the Alps to the north and the Mediterranean Sea to the south. The city itself was bordered by the river on one side, and the fact that they were on a hill meant that they had a safe defensive position as well.

The Latins in the area were bordered by the Greeks in the south, who brought with them education, reading and writing, and religion, all of which heavily influenced Roman civilization. For instance, the Roman gods Jupiter, Mars and Venus are the Greek gods Zeus, Ares, and Aphrodite respectively.

To the north were the Etruscans, who the Romans saw as extravagant, dishonest and weak. The Etruscans crossed the river Tiber and settled in Latium (the region of Italy where Rome was founded) in around 650-600 BC, leading many archaeologists to speculate that this was the reason why the settlement on Palatine hill joined the ones on the surrounding hills.

The Roman scholar and writer Marcus Terentius Varro suggested that the city was founded on the 21 of April 753 BC. This suggestion was widely accepted by the Romans and is still accepted by scholars today.

The beginning of Rome saw the beginning of one of the most politically diverse civilizations ever, and this political diversity is what we shall examine in the next chapter.

Chapter 2:
The Roman Kingdom

The Roman civilization had three primary systems of government in the twelve centuries that it existed, a Monarchy that lasted from 753 BC to 509 BC, a Republic that existed between 509 BC and 27 BC, and an Autocratic Empire that lasted from 27 BC to the fall of the last emperor Romulus Augustus in 476 AD.

The Kingdoms

The Roman kingdom is the period in which the monarchical system of government ruled the ancient civilization. Few written records have survived from the era, and the records that do exist were written during the time of the Republic or the Empire and are primarily based on legends. However, they do begin at the same time, 753 BC, and all of them list seven kings that ruled the city between its inception and the fall of the last king. Roman kings, other than Romulus, were elected to the throne and did not gain it by right.

The seven kings are listed below, in the order in which they ruled the city.

Romulus

The first king of Rome and its mythical founder, Romulus is accredited with starting the Senate. In an effort to increase the population of the city, Romulus allowed men of all classes to come to Rome as citizens. However, the influx of men caused an imbalance, as there were not enough women in his city for the men to marry.

To rectify the situation, Romulus held a massive celebration for the festival of Consus (the god of the granary and the storehouse) and invited the neighboring tribes to attend. The festival was ended abruptly as the Romans kidnaped the neighboring Sabines' unmarried women and took them as wives. The resulting war led to Romulus and the Sabine king Titus Tatius agreeing to rule the two factions together as one kingdom. This joined rule lasted until the death of Titus Tatius, who left Romulus to rule the city on his own.

Numa Pompilius

After the death of Romulus, a Sabine religious and cultural figure, Numa Pompilius, was elected king. He is credited with moving the vestal virgins from Alba Longa to Rome, and with starting various priestly colleges. Numa Pompilius is considered the father of Roman culture, successfully turning the semi-barbaric Roman citizens into something resembling a civilization.

Tullus Hostilius

This bloodthirsty king was unlike his predecessor in many ways, and because of it, he saw two major wars in 31-year reign. However, towards the end of his reign, Rome was struck by a plague and he changed his ways, seeking to avert the wrath of the gods. However, it did not work, and soon after, he was killed by a bolt of lightning that struck his home and set it ablaze.

Ancus Marcius

Rome's fourth king and Numa Pompilius' grandson, Ancus Marcius was elected to bring back the peace and prosperity that the Romans had enjoyed during his grandfather's reign.

He was tested by the *Prisci Latini*, who he defeated and assimilated into the growing Roman population. He is credited with building the port of Ostia and Rome's first prison on Capitoline Hill.

Lucius Tarquinius Priscus (Lucius Tarquinius the Elder)

The first king of Etruscan birth, Lucius Tarquinius Priscus conquered the remaining Sabines and Etruscans, doubling the size of Rome. He also built the Cloaca Maxima, Rome's first sewer system, and the Circus Maximus in which he staged the games he had created.

Servius Tullius

Servius Tullius was the second king of Etruscan birth and Lucius Tarquinius' son-in-law. He had various achievements including building the first wall to encircle the seven hills of Rome, as well as initiating the Roman Census and changing legislation so that voting rights were now according to socio-economic status. The change in the law meant that the plebeians (commoners) could now share some of the same rights as the patricians (the aristocracy).

Lucius Tarquinius Superbus (Lucius Tarquinius the Proud)

The last king of Rome and the son of Tarquinius Priscus, he cemented Rome's place as the head of the Latin cities during his reign. He also continued works on the Circus Maximus, Cloaca Maxima and the temple of Jupiter.

His son, Sextus Tarquinius raped Lucretia, the wife and daughter of some Roman patricians. This sparked a rebellion that saw Tarquinius Superbus and his family forced into exile in 509 BC. The roman word for king "Rex" was viewed in a negative light from that point on until the decline of the empire almost 1,000 years later.

Chapter 3: The Republic

After the fall of Tarquinius Superbus, the new office of Consul was created. This new position was first filled by the leaders of the 509 BC rebellion, Lucius Junius Brutus, and Lucius Tarquinius Collatinus. The consul was appointed every year and had all the original powers that the king had, except that power was shared amongst two people who could veto each other.

However, the powers were slowly stripped from the Consuls, first by adding other magistrates that also held portions of the king's power. After the consul came the Praetor, who dealt with legal and judicial matters, and the Censor, who conducted the Roman census. The other magistrates were the Tribunes, who were chosen by the plebeians to represent them, the Quaestors who were in charge of public revenue and Aediles who had a range of responsibilities, from public buildings to the supply of grain to the city.

The Early Republic

The early republic was full of conflicts as the Romans sought to adjust to their independence and expand their borders. First Collatinus was exiled because he was a direct descendant of the fallen monarch, then Brutus died while defending Rome from an attempt by Tarquinius Superbus to regain his throne. The Etruscans then took over the city for a while, but they were defeated by citizens of the other cities in Latium. There was then a series of internal conflict, but the Romans overcame them and finally conquered the Italian peninsula in around 272 BC.

One of the most notable conflicts of the time was the conflict of orders. In 494 BC, Rome was at war with two neighboring tribes. The plebeian soldiers refused to defend the city unless they were given the right to elect their own leaders (the Tribunes). The patricians agreed, and the soldiers went back to the battlefield and defeated their enemies.

The first plebeian praetor was elected in 337 BC, sparking improved relations between the Tribunes and the Senators. It was around this time that the plebeians were finally allowed to sit in the senate though it was still hard to get in if you were not from a political family.

The plebeians may have been gaining equality in the senate, but they were still destitute. In 287 BC, after the Senators refused to grant them relief from their suffering they retreated to Janiculum hill and refused to return. A dictator was appointed to help mediate between the two factions, which resulted in him passing a law stating that the patrician senators no longer need to agree on a bill before it is discussed in the plebeian council.

This move meant that the power had finally shifted from the patricians to the plebian politicians. However, the politicians soon lost interest in the plight of the average plebeian, and they rebelled again. This time, they left Rome entirely, and only returned when their demands for equal rights were accepted.

The First and Second Triumvirate

Towards the end of the republic, the Triumvirate appeared. This was a political alliance between the three most prominent Roman leaders of the time. The first Triumvirate consisted of

Gnaeus Pompeius Magnus, also known as Pompey the Great, Gaius Julius Caesar, and Marcus Licinius Crassus.

According to their agreement, Julius Caesar would be consul in 59 BC, and then serve as governor of Gail for five years, Pompey would have his treaties sanctioned, and Crassus would be made consul in the future. However, by 56 BC the political ties between the three were straining. In 53 BC they were dealt a crushing blow when Caesar's daughter Julia, who was also Pompey's wife, died in childbirth, and Crassus died in battle.

The following year saw Pompey elected consul though his politicking led to a civil war in 49 BC. Pompey lost the war to Julius Caesar and was subsequently murdered in Egypt, leaving Caesar, the sole leader of Rome.

The second Triumvirate was established by Gaius Octavius, Marcus Lepidus and Mark Anthony in late 43 BC and is widely viewed as the beginning of the decline of the Roman Republic. Unlike the last Triumvirate, this one was a legally established institution and took over after the assassination of Caesar. They were opposed by the senate, which resulted in the death of the rebel senators, Marcus Junius Brutus and Gaius Cassius Longinus at Philippi in 42 BC.

Marc Anthony and Gaius Octavian, Caesar's adopted son, then fought each other. Marc Anthony was finally defeated at the Battle of Actium, and he and his lover Cleopatra committed suicide rather than face capture. This left Gaius Octavius as the sole ruler of Rome, who returned to Rome, accepted the title Augustus meaning "Exalted One" and became the first Emperor of Rome.

Chapter 4: Building the Empire

The Roman Empire is considered to have started in 27 BC when Gaius Octavius (also called Octavian) took the name Augustus and assumed absolute power. The government officially remained a republic, but with time, the Emperors destroyed the republican values.

Four principal dynasties ruled the empire from its creation to its eventual demise.

The Julio-Claudian Dynasty

This dynasty was established by Augustus and was called the Julio-Claudian dynasty due to the family of Augustus (called Julia) and the family of Tiberius (called Claudia). The dynasty had five emperors, Augustus, Tiberius, Caligula, Claudius, and Nero. The most successful rulers of this dynasty are Augustus and Claudius, who are seen as very successful politicians and military commanders. Caligula and Nero, however, are seen as dysfunctional and slightly mad.

Caesar Augustus absorbed all the republican power he could under his official title of *princeps*. He was the Consul, *princeps senatus (Senate leader),* Aedile, censor and tribune. He also named himself *"Imperator Gaius Julius Caesar Divi Filius"* or "Commander Gaius Julius Caesar, son of the deified", boasting about his link to the deified Julius Caesar, and using the term Imperator to permanently link himself to the roman tradition of victory.

Augustus' reign saw Rome experience peace and prosperity with significant advances made in literature and an expansion of the empire's borders. He also continued making changes to the calendar that Julius Caesar had started, and the month August is named after him.

The dynasty ruled until the death of Nero in 68 AD. Tiberius was not politically driven and agreed with the senate when they suggested he retire to Capri in 26 AD. He died there 11 years later in 37 AD and was succeeded by Caligula, his grandnephew as his grandson Tiberius Gemellus was still a child at the time of his death.

Caligula became insane during his reign and is reported as having nominated a horse to be consul at one point. However, his insanity was not tolerated for long, and he was murdered by the Praetorian Guard in 41 AD. His uncle Claudius took over as emperor though he was also assassinated soon after he took the throne, this time by his wife Agrippina the younger, whose son Nero became emperor.

Nero was the first persecutor of Christians, and he faced many revolts in his time. He committed suicide in 68 AD after a revolt of the senate led by Servius Sulpicius Galba.

Flavian Dynasty

After the death of Nero, four different emperors ruled Rome in one year. This time is popularly known as the Year of Four Emperors. The four emperors were:

- Galba, who was killed by the praetorian guard
- Otho, who committed suicide after being defeated in the Battle of Bedriacum
- Vitellius, who was killed by Vespasian's men after the second Battle of Bedriacum

- Vespasian, who founded the Flavian Dynasty

Vespasian completed construction on many incomplete buildings in his time as Emperor and reconstructed buildings that had been burned during the great fire of Rome. He also began construction on the coliseum and extended the British territory. He died in 79 AD as was succeeded by his son Titus.

Titus completed the coliseum and encouraged the games that would be played there for the next 100 years. He also continued the expansion of the Roman Empire, but his conquests were cut short when he died of fever in 81 AD after just 2 years as emperor. His brother Domitian succeeded him and went on to rule for 15 years. Domitian fancied himself as the next Augustus ad was known to compare himself to the gods. This behavior angered the patricians, who finally assassinated him in 96 AD.

Chapter 5:
The Peak and Beginnings of Decline

The Nerva-Antonine Dynasty

This dynasty ruled at the height of the Roman Empire when the civilization was at its peak both territorially and economically. It saw the return of peace and prosperity to the region, and the reinstatement of the senator's right to choose an emperor, which had not been done since Octavius was given the title Augustus in 27 BC.

They chose Nerva, a man with noble ties who had served Emperor Nero and the Flavian Dynasty. He restored many of the liberties that Domitian had taken away and by the time of his death in 98 AD, the Roman Empire was so stable the transition between emperors was peaceful for the first time in decades.

His heir was his adopted son Trajan, who was a successful military general. Trajan ruled in the same way that Nerva did, freeing those that had been wrongfully imprisoned by Domitian and returning private property that was confiscated by the fallen emperor. Trajan also conquered Dacia, Armenia, and Mesopotamia, and by the time of his death in 117 AD, the Roman Empire had reached the peak of its territorial expansion.

Before his death, Trajan named Hadrian his successor. Hadrian avoided war even more than his predecessors did, and not only did he withdraw troops from Mesopotamia, he also built the famous Hadrian's wall in northern Britain to keep the barbaric northern tribes out of Roman Britain. He also built many aqueducts, baths, libraries and theaters and abolished torture during his reign. He died in 138 AD, having visited nearly every province in the empire.

Hadrian was succeeded by Antonius Pius, who built temples, theaters, and mausoleums. He promoted philosophy, the arts and sciences. He expanded Roman Britain, conquering the south of Scotland and building the Antonine wall, which was completed in 154 AD. He was succeeded by Marcus Aurelius in 161 AD after his death.

Marcus Aurelius was a philosopher and an author who is famous not only for being a Roman Emperor, but also for writing the series of books Meditations which he used as a kind of self-improvement guide. He defeated the Parthian Empire and successfully defended Rome from various barbaric tribes during the Marcomannic wars.

The Nerva-Antonine dynasty is considered the golden age of the Roman Empire, with five of its emperors being nicknamed the "Five Good Emperors" by Niccolo Machiavelli in 1503. The Roman population of this time enjoyed all the benefits of living in a prosperous nation, and the senate appeared to regain some of its power. By the time Marcus Aurelius' son Commodus was becoming emperor, the empire seemed like it may last forever.

Severan Dynasty

Commodus was murdered in late 192 AD, and what followed was the Year of Five Emperors. Like in the Year of Four Emperors, this year saw five different emperors vie for the throne though only one managed to keep it. Pertinax, Didius Julianus, Pescennius Niger, Septimius Severus, and Claudius Albinus all fought for the throne. After many battles, Septimius Severus was finally named Emperor of Rome.

Severus was unlike the six emperors that had ruled before him because he loved war and violence. He declared war on Parthia after they tried to invade Roman Territory and captured the Parthian capital of Ctesiphon in 164 AD. He intended to annihilate the whole of Britain by waging war with the Caledonians, but his attempts failed when he fell ill and died in 211 AD.

Severus was succeeded by his two sons, Caracalla, and Geta. Caracalla had Geta assassinated soon after he came to power so that he could rule the empire by himself. He continued in his father's war-like footsteps and gained the respect of his legions.

However, Caracalla was a cruel man who once ordered that the population of Alexandria be eliminated because they did not like him. He killed most of the people of the city in 215 AD, but this cruelty was not to last. In 217 AD, Caracalla was assassinated by one of his own soldiers while on a campaign in Parthia.

The Praetorian Prefect Macrinus, who ordered Caracalla's demise succeeded him for a short while but was ousted from power in 218 AD by Elagabalus, a relative of the Severi. Elagabalus proved to be an extravagant emperor and books such as the Historia Augusta and writers like Herodian all bear witness to his waste.

Elagabalus was succeeded by his cousin Alexander Severus, who mounted numerous campaigns against various, such as the Persians and the Germans that had invaded Gaul. However, his lack of victories on the battlefield did not sit well with his soldiers, and he was assassinated by his own soldiers in 235 AD.

The death of Alexander marked the end of the Severan Dynasty and the beginning of the period called Crisis of the Third Century. This period saw a series of civil wars that resulted in the empire proclaiming 26 Emperors in a 49-year period.

Some form of stability was restored in 284 AD when Diocletian was declared Imperator by the eastern army. At this time, a new form of government was introduced that actually split the empire into two. It was called the Tetrarchy, and it divided the empire between 4 emperors, two in the east and two in the west. Diocletian and Galerius ruled in the east while Maximian and Flavius Constantinus ruled in the west.

The Eastern Empire was responsible for a majority of the Christian persecution from around 303 AD to 305 AD. Diocletian abdicated in 305 AD, making him the first emperor in to resign. His reign however, ended the traditional Imperial Roman rule the Principate (The First, from princeps), and replaced it with the Dominate (Master), as Diocletian unlike the rest of the Roman Emperors did not pretend that the roman republic still existed.

Diocletian was succeeded by Constantine, who waged war against the other tetrarchs and finally succeeded in reuniting the civilization under one emperor again. He allowed Christians to worship freely, and he converted to Christianity. His biggest achievement though is the reconstruction of Byzantium, which he renamed Nova Roma. The city became informally known as Constantinople (City of Constantine), and it remained the Roman capital until the fall of the Western Empire in 1453 when it was conquered by the Ottoman Empire.

Conclusion

The fall of the Roman Empire has been debated for centuries. Some scholars say that it was not really a decline, as even though the political and military system of the empire was destroyed, some of the cultural and political aspects of the civilization remained after 476 AD. The retention of some of these ideas has led some historians to state that the empire underwent a cultural transformation rather than a complete decline into oblivion.

Other historians dispute the fall of the empire because even though the empire may have lost its legitimacy in 476, Constantinople was not conquered until almost 1000 years later in 1453, when the Ottoman Empire finally captured the city and made it their capital.

Whatever the case may be the steady decline of power that the Roman government faced in the 100 years between 376 and 476 AD was real, and led to the eventual disintegration of the empire into various smaller kingdoms and city-states.

Despite this, it is widely accepted that the Roman Civilization is the ancestor of western civilization. The alphabet, culture, law, religion, technology, architecture, political system, military, government, and languages of the western world can be traced back to the Roman Empire in one way or another.

The rediscovery of the Roman Civilization in the 14th to 17th centuries is thought to be a significant influence on the renaissance and the age of enlightenment. This just shows that even after millennia, the Roman culture still has the power to influence millions.

Printed in Great Britain
by Amazon.co.uk, Ltd.,
Marston Gate.